TEACH AND REACH

TEACH
AND
REACH

Joseph Fielding McConkie

Bookcraft
SALT LAKE CITY, UTAH

Library of Congress Catalog Card Number: 75-31080
ISBN 0-88494-289-9

2nd Printing, 1987

Lithographed in the United States of America
PUBLISHERS PRESS
Salt Lake City, Utah

*To my mother Amelia S. McConkie
and my wife Brenda —
both exemplary teachers of
spiritual truths*

CONTENTS

PREFACE

As a teacher I make no profession to having all the answers, but rather to having struggled with many of the questions and problems. I have written not of the teacher that I am, but of the teacher that I desire to become; the kind of teacher at whose feet I thrill to sit and with whom I long to entrust the precious souls of my own children.

To teach the gospel of Jesus Christ is a sacred privilege. It is my hope that everything within the covers of this book partakes of that spirit and is in harmony with truth.

Chapter One

CORRECT PRINCIPLES
OF GOSPEL TEACHING

When the storm abates and the skies clear, the mariner who has been tossed at sea can, by calculating his relationship to fixed stars, again establish his bearings and check his course. In like manner, those commissioned to teach the gospel of Jesus Christ need to regularly verify their course. Like the mariner, they, too, utilize the principles of celestial navigation, checking their course against eternal principles which do not vary. Correct principles, like the miraculous directors given by the Lord to Lehi, announce a clear course according to the faith, diligence, and heed which we give them. As the sailor must be familiar with his sextant, and the explorer his compass, we, as teachers, must be familiar with those principles that establish the direction of our journey. Perhaps an appropriate beginning, then, to an essay on the divine stewardship of gospel teachers would be to briefly identify the basic principles which establish our course and determine our direction.

Salvation Founded in Truth

Some have advocated the marriage of faith and reason. Yet marriages sought to cement alliances between foreign kingdoms rarely result in true happiness. The offspring of such unions often find themselves torn between conflicting loyalties and estranged by both societies.

It has been correctly observed that the theology that weds itself to the ethics of the day will be a widow in the succeeding generation. Though the ceremony can be mocked, an eternal union can only be entered into upon eternal principles. Ethical systems do not profess the power to save or exalt man, and we should not append such hopes to them. "Earthly and heavenly philosophy are two different things, and it is folly for men to base their arguments upon earthly philosophy in trying to unravel the mysteries of the Kingdom of God."[1]

Simply stated, there is no salvation in ignorance or error. Theories and philosophies cannot save. Salvation is found in Christ and his gospel. As beneficial as it may be to learn the things of the world, eternal blessings come only through revealed knowledge. The knowledge that saves is the knowledge of God. If our objective is to save men, we need not add to that revealed knowledge the philosophies of men or the so-called wisdom of the ages. As the Prophet Joseph Smith said, "One truth revealed from heaven is worth all the sectarian notions in existence."[2]

God, and all truths associated with him, stands revealed or remains forever unknown. Salvation is founded in revealed religion. Such truths are absolute and eternal; they are not in flux; they do not vary. What is true in one age is true in every age. The gospel truths by which Abraham, Isaac, and Jacob gained their exaltation are the same truths by which we must gain ours. No scientific discovery will ever set at naught the plan of salvation, nor need we expect the possibility of a new revelation that dispenses with faith, repentance, baptism, or any other part of that eternal plan. The principles that save are everlastingly the same. Such truths bow to no man and seek alliances with none. Such truths are not determined by the mind of man nor weighed and measured by his ability to reason.

No Salvation in Partial Truths or Partial Acceptance

Many of the Church's programs are being imitated by the

---

1. John Taylor, *Journal of Discourses,* 26 vols. (London: Latter-day Saints' Book Depot, 1884), 14:191; hereafter cited as *JD.*

2. *History of the Church of Jesus Christ of Latter-day Saints,* ed. B. H. Roberts, 7 vols., 2d ed. rev. (Salt Lake City: Deseret Book Co., 1949), 6:252; hereafter cited as *HC.*

world. We, in fact, encourage them to do so. We anxiously tell people about our programs and supply them with manuals and testimonials. The pivotal question, however, is "Can you really operate the programs if you do not believe in the eternal principles of which they are but a manifestation?" The plain answer is that you cannot. To accept a program but reject its founding principles has been likened to allowing your children to receive all their immunization shots as long as no serum is used in the needle, and then to act surprised when the injection fails to protect them from the effects of the dreaded diseases.

The Brethren have emphasized to us that the vitality of Mormonism is in its theology, not in its programs.[3] This principle is illustrated by the two Catholic priests who came into my office to learn how to operate the family home evening program. My colleagues and I explained the Church's program, answered their questions, gave them encouragement, and supplied them with a home evening manual. We sent them away in the hope that the program will be a help to the families of their parish, but in the realization that it will not save the Catholic Church or its members.

A testimony of the programs of the Church and active participation in them is not sufficient to save. The Church is more than an effective social club and we must be more than card-carrying members. Many good people standing outside the Church express a profound respect for the programs of the Church and the fruits that flow from them. I have acquaintance with a wealthy man who has contributed liberally to support these programs, and though he wants his family to partake of the fruits of the gospel, he denies its divine origin. He has no belief in God or hope for life after death. He will be and has been blessed for his financial support of the Church, but his testimony of the programs of the Church will not excuse him from the effects of eternal laws. For it is only by obedience to eternal laws that men are saved.

Our commitment must be to all the doctrines and instructions that come through the channels the Lord has ordained for that purpose. We cannot accept the principle of faith and reject

the principle of repentance. We cannot accept the principle of repentance and reject baptism. We cannot accept the programs of the Church and reject the eternal principles upon which they are based. Nor is it our right to pick and choose between gospel principles; their validity is not based on our likes or dislikes. There is no salvation in partial truths or in partial acceptance of the truth.

No Acceptable Substitutes for Truth

There are no acceptable substitutes for truth. "Faith comes by hearing the word of God, [as it is taught] through the testimony of the servants of God."[4] Philosophy, ethics, and the wisdom of the world are not the only synthetics offered under a gospel label. Many inservice programs get lost in methodology and rarely concern themselves with what is being taught as long as it is being taught well. Teachers who are the products of such training often find themselves giving beautifully packaged gifts which when opened are of slight or passing worth. Might we ask of what value it is if a teacher has high involvement, good discipline, a neat and orderly classroom, but never really teaches anything? What is the value of a well-told story if it carries no message? If that which matters most is not to be at the mercy of that which matters least, the *how* of teaching cannot relegate the *what* of teaching to a place of secondary importance.

The Measure of Methodology

The salvation of teaching is not to be found in the mechanics of methodology. The greatest discourses and lessons in this world's history have been accomplished without the benefit of behavior objectives, educational games, audio-visual devices, maps, pictures, filmstrips, chalkboards, or even a classroom. The greatness of Christ's teachings were to be found within himself. He had a perfect knowledge of that which he taught and of those whom he taught. Allegories, similes, parables, irony, logic, scripture, revelation, and testimony all flowed freely from his lips. Christ's teaching aids

4. *HC,* 3:379.

were unrehearsed, unplanned, and unsophisticated. They were spontaneous, simple, and direct. His mind and soul being a great repository of the words of life, in each instance he was able to have given to him that portion that he in turn was to mete out to every man. Lacking that repository of understanding, teachers are often tempted to turn to timefillers to get themselves "off the hook." Gimmicks and games with younger groups and class discussions or debates with adult classes are commonly substituted for proper preparation and inspiration.

It is not my intent to condemn teaching devices, but rather to qualify the manner in which they are used. The value of all things is in proper use. The measuring rod of methodology is in how it enhances the teaching of truth. Without question, teaching devices have their place, but that place must be determined on sound and clearly understood principles. It is when they are used as camouflage for lazy teachers that such devices get a bad reputation. Students who have been dined on a seven-course meal of fried fluff may have enjoyed the sweetness of its taste, but they soon find that such a meal does not produce sufficient spiritual energy to sustain them when strength is needed.

Truths Through the Spirit

By revelation the Lord has announced his own philosophy of education. (D&C 50:11-20.) With the announcement that he would reason as a man reasons, he commenced to ask and answer a series of questions:

Question: "Wherefore, I the Lord ask you this question — unto what were ye ordained?"

Answer: "To preach my gospel by the Spirit, even the Comforter which was sent forth to teach the truth."

We note, then, that the ordination, the commission, or the call, is to go forth to "teach the truth." Nothing more, nothing less. The manner in which the truth is to be taught is "by the Spirit," or with the aid of the Comforter. Now, to insure that the message has been understood, the Lord asks another question:

Question: "Verily I say unto you, he that is ordained of me and sent forth to preach the word of truth by the Comforter, in the Spirit of truth, doth he preach it by the Spirit of truth or some other way?"

The Lord, then, is suggesting that "it," meaning the "word of truth," can be taught "some other way" than by the Spirit. Should that happen, the Lord says: "And if it be by some other way it is not of God."

The concept is a companion to one announced in an earlier revelation wherein the Lord said: "If ye receive not the Spirit ye shall not teach." (D&C 42:14.) Even pure truth taught independent of the Spirit is not acceptable to God. Though I, as a teacher, may go into the classroom and teach nothing but truth, if I do so on my own without the sustaining direction of the Spirit, the Lord rejects it as not being of him. So though I have gone through the right motions, said the right things, and quoted the right passages, drawn the right conclusions, and given correct counsel, no true spiritual learning has taken place and hence I have not taught. Cognitively all that I have done is correct; spiritually it is not.

But one might ask, "Can truth be taught independent of the Spirit?" Our answer is "Yes." Satan can and does teach truth. Never an iota more, to be sure, than he has to in order to deceive, but we must recognize that his great mastery is in his ability to mingle truth and error. How else could he challenge the very elect?

We live in a world in which synthetics are commonplace: logic and reason, argument and debate, science and archeology, charisma and humor have all at one time or another been used as substitutes for the Spirit in teaching the gospel. This is not to say that these methods should never be used in the classrooms of the Church, but that irrespective of how effectively they are used, they will not result in the testimony that saves unless they are used under the direction of the Spirit.

In the revelation on how the gospel should be taught, the Lord also defined the responsibility and role of the student of the gospel. Again he did so in question and answer form:

Question: "And again, he that receiveth the word of truth, doth he receive it by the Spirit of truth or some other way?"

Answer: "If it be some other way it is not of God." (D&C 50:19-20.)

The doctrine that the Lord previously announced for teachers of the gospel is now applied to the gospel student. They, too, must get the Spirit. They, too, can gain a gospel understanding "some other way" and are warned that such "is not of God." The knowledge of spiritual things must be both taught and learned by the Spirit.

The Path of Truth

Mormonism advocates no new principles. We set our course by following the same principles as did the saints anciently. We traverse the same seas, we follow the same stars, we pursue the same destination; for as Nephi of old declared: "This is the way; and there is none other." (2 Ne. 31:21.) Ours is not a bargain basement theology; we offer no sales, we have no gimmicks, we have found no new and easy way. Our course is set. It is the path of truth, a path from which we cannot depart in safety — a path from which there are no shortcuts.

Chapter 2

A TEACHER'S DIVINE COMMISSION

It is a sacred right to teach the gospel of Jesus Christ. A right not granted to men generally. A right reserved to those called and commissioned by him whose gospel it is. And, as with all commissions, the divine stewardship of teachers has been granted only within established bounds and limits, which are attended by that wisdom that finds its origin in the mind of God. As spelled out by revelation, the commission of gospel teachers may be broken down into the following parts: "first, seek to obtain my word" (D&C 11:21); second, "teach the principles of my gospel, [third,] which are in the Bible and the Book of Mormon" (D&C 42:12); fourth, " as . . . directed by the Spirit" (D&C 42:13); fifth, "liken them [the scriptures] unto yourselves." (1 Ne. 19:24); sixth, seal your teachings with the testimony that the doctrines you have taught are true. (Alma 5:45.) Let us briefly consider each of these facets of a teacher's commission.

"First Seek to Obtain My Word"

We cannot teach that which we do not know. We cannot testify to that of which we are not witnesses. Not only is a mastery of the subject matter an essential to effective teaching, it is a prerequisite to having the Spirit. In the realm of spiritual

things a man can no more reap where he has not sown than he can in the realm of physical things. The right to draw upon the spirit is earned, just as confidence and understanding are earned.

When Hyrum Smith as a young man sought for the right to go forth as a gospel teacher, the Lord responded, "Seek not to declare my word, but first seek to obtain my word." (D&C 11:21.) When Hyrum had paid the price in study and preparation, the Lord promised him that his tongue would be loosed and that he would have the Spirit, the knowledge, and "the power of God unto the convincing of men." (Ibid.) This experience illustrates the inseparable relationship between personal preparation, having the Spirit, and the subsequent "power of God unto the convincing of men." It was nearly a year later that the Lord, speaking again to Hyrum Smith, said: "Behold, I speak unto you, Hyrum, a few words; for thou also art under no condemnation, and thy heart is opened, and thy tongue loosed; and thy calling is to exhortation, and to strengthen the Church continually." (D&C 23:3.)

Teach Gospel Principles

Integrity demands that employees do the work for which they are employed. Suppose that as the chairman of the department of music at a university you discovered that one of your instructors in that college was teaching mathematics for a curriculum in his music classes. When you called him to account for his activities, he argued that he was a brilliant mathematician, that all he had taught was true, that his students enjoyed his classes, and that he had frequently shown them the relationships between mathematics and music.

Despite all the good things that could be said about the instructor's class in mathematics, he had been employed to teach music and had no right to do otherwise. Similarly, the Lord expects those commissioned to teach his gospel to teach his gospel and not another. No matter how rational and brilliant their personal philosophies may be, they have no more right to teach those philosophies than they have to sow seeds of doubt or discord or to modify or change the Lord's gospel in any

way. Their commission is to teach the gospel, not to change the gospel.

In the broadest sense all truth is part of the gospel, and in that general sense the commission of a gospel teacher could be viewed as the right to teach anything that is true. However, in the higher spiritual sense, in which the term is used in the revelations, the gospel is concerned with and defined as those particular truths by conformity to which men can sanctify themselves and work out their salvation. Neal A. Maxwell has pointed out that there is no democracy among truths; they are not all of the same worth. Scripturally, truth has been defined as a "knowledge of things as they are, and as they were, and as they are to come." (D&C 93:24.) Three time-lines are suggested: past, present, and future. The commission of gospel teachers is in the realm of those truths that span all three time-lines. Those laws, doctrines, ordinances, powers, and authorities which remain the same yesterday, today, and forever are the principles that constitute a teacher's divine commission.

The Lord's directive to his missionaries is "of tenets thou shalt not talk, but thou shalt declare repentance and faith on the Savior, and remission of sins by baptism, and by fire, yea, even the Holy Ghost." (D&C 19:31.) By definition tenets are principles, dogmas, doctrines, and beliefs. If correctly understood and taught, they are true yet they do not fall within the bounds of a missionary's commission. The charge given to missionaries is to teach specific truths (the basic principles) and not to teach others. In a like manner, gospel teachers are sent into the classroom with a specific charge as to what they are to teach.

This is not to say that manuals and course outlines in the Church are inviolable. Teachers are always expected to follow the Spirit and depart from lesson materials as it is appropriate. One can depart from a lesson outline without departing from the lesson objective. One can depart from a lesson on a particular gospel principle without departing from gospel principles. One can depart from a Book of Mormon manual without departing from the Book of Mormon and its great messages.

Again, if the commission the Lord has given to his missionaries is applicable to classroom teachers, they should teach "none other things than that which the prophets and apostles have written, and that which is taught them by the Comforter through the prayer of faith." (D&C 52:9.)

Teach from the Scriptures

On many occasions I have listened to people tell stories about things my father or grandfather is supposed to have said or done which I know are not true. I have occasionally listened with surprise to things I am said to have taught or done that also have little or no resemblance to what, in fact, did happen. In most of these instances the stories or expressions have been given in good faith, without any desire to distort or pervert truth. Yet, through them, I have learned the importance of being cautious about second- and third-hand accounts of what people have supposedly said or done. The teachings of Christ, in a like manner, have been subject to the same distortions.

This is a problem to which all gospel teachers should be sensitive. An original source, when available, is always preferable to a secondary source. Certainly the words of Christ should be preferred over someone else's expression as to what the words of Christ are. Appropriately, the commission to teach the gospel also specifies the source from which it is to be taught — the scriptures themselves. What better source is there from which to preach the word of the Lord than the voice of the Lord? Of the scriptures the Lord has said: "These words are not of men nor of man, but of me . . . it is my voice which speaketh them unto you; for they are given by my Spirit unto you, and by my power you can read them one to another. . . . Wherefore, you can testify that you have heard my voice, and know my words." (D&C 18:34-36.)

The question is frequently asked, "What is the best commentary on the scriptures?" to which a most appropriate answer is "The scriptures themselves." For instance, what an unfortunate thing it would be if a gospel teacher turned to sectarian commentaries for an explanation of the New Testament parables, when Christ, the author of those very parables

has given his explanation in the Doctrine and Covenants, an explanation which is very much at variance with those of the commentators. Certainly one would not want to teach the Old Testament without the aid of the Pearl of Great Price with its amplified and inspired teachings about Adam, Enoch, Moses, and Abraham. How unfortunate it would be to have members of the Church study Isaiah without the aid of the Book of Mormon and the Doctrine and Covenants. One-third of the book of Isaiah is quoted in the Book of Mormon, much of it with interpretation and commentary by the Book of Mormon prophets. This makes the Book of Mormon the finest commentary on Isaiah known to man. Second only to the Book of Mormon would be the Doctrine and Covenants, which contains revealed interpretations along with approximately one hundred instances in which is quoted, paraphrased, or interpreted the language of Isaiah.

The parables and the book of Isaiah are but two of a host of illustrations that could be given. The essential point is that nothing could be more natural than to find Christ, who revealed his truths anciently, revealing those same truths today and doing so in a manner which intertwines his words, ancient and modern, so that they literally fulfill his prophecy that they would become one in the hand of gospel teachers. (Ezek. 37:17.) The best commentary on the scriptures is always the scriptures themselves. It takes a prophet to understand a prophet, revelation to understand revelation, and the scriptures to understand the scriptures.

In the United States, fixed standards for weight and measurement have been established by Congress. These standards, in turn, were derived from prototypes kept at an international bureau of weights and measures located near Paris, France. The standardization of weights and measures makes it possible for all participating countries to exchange goods, services, data, and all manner of information in an equitable, understandable, and orderly manner. Similarly, a universal standard has been established whereby men can get a correct measurement of truth. That source is referred to as the standard works, by which is meant the Bible, Book of Mormon, Doctrine and Covenants, and Pearl of Great Price. These four volumes are

the measuring rods or standards by which all doctrines, philosophies, theories, or views can be judged.

"The truth of all things is measured by the scriptures. That which harmonizes with them should be accepted; that which is contrary to their teachings, however plausible it may seem for the moment, will not endure and should be rejected.

"The books, writings, explanations, expositions, views, and theories of even the wisest and greatest men, either in or out of the Church, do not rank with the standard works. Even the writings, teachings, and opinions of the prophets of God are acceptable only to the extent they are in harmony with what God has revealed and what is recorded in the standard works. When the living oracles speak in the name of the Lord or as moved upon by the Holy Ghost, however, their utterances are then binding upon all who hear, and whatever is said will without any exception be found to be in harmony with the standard works. The Lord's house is a house of order, and one truth never contradicts another." [1]

Teach by the Spirit

"I had only traveled a short time to testify to the people," said Brigham Young, "before I learned this one fact, that you might prove doctrine from the Bible till doomsday, and it would merely convince a people but would not convert them. You might read the Bible from Genesis to Revelation and prove every iota that you advance, and that alone would have no converting influence upon the people. Nothing short of a testimony by the power of the Holy Ghost would bring light and knowledge to them — bring them in their hearts to repentance. Nothing short of that would ever do." [2]

Since all true religion is revealed religion, the commission of gospel teachers is to teach and testify of those revealed truths. Their commission is not in the realm of reason and intellect, though without question all spiritual truths are in

---

1. Bruce R. McConkie, *Mormon Doctrine*, 2d ed. rev. (Salt Lake City: Bookcraft, 1966), p. 765.
2. *JD*, 5:327.

perfect accord with all intellectual realities. Yet the things of God are known only by the Spirit of God. The commission of a gospel teacher, therefore, does not embrace the right to argue, debate, or partake of the spirit of contention. They are to be actuated by a spirit of humility and their language is to be meek. In fact, they have been expressly forbidden from bringing "railing accusation" even against the legions of the adversary. (D&C 50:33.) Gospel principles were intended to be taught in simplicity by the Spirit, and, as noted in the preceding chapter, to rely on any other spirit or approach is to do that which is not of God. (D&C 50:11-22.)

Liken Scriptures unto Yourselves

Nephi, giving the key as to how scriptures can be effectively taught, said, "For I did liken all scriptures unto us," explaining that he did so in order that it might be for their "profit and learning." (1 Ne. 19:23-24.) The scriptures are alive with characters and events that translate themselves easily into modern settings. Who has never, Enoch-like, at least felt like protesting a call to service with a "Why me?" attitude. "[I] am but a lad," Enoch argued, "[unpopular and] slow of speech. (Moses 6:31.) Who has never experienced Jonah-like indignation when someone repents whom we did not expect to? (Jonah 4.) Our own Church history is full of the political tyranny and villainy of Pharaohs, Herods, and Pilates; and is not the world still full of people who, Nicodemus-like, privately and quietly seek after the Church but publicly shun it?

Are there no more doubting Thomases or impetuous Peters who dare rebuke the Lord? (Matt. 16:22.) Or Amuleks who know the gospel is true but will not know it, who have heard the voice of the Lord but will not hear it? (Alma 10:5-6.) Are there no more Professor Korihors who tell us that our religion consists of the "foolish traditions" of our fathers, that we cannot know of things we cannot see, that all religious belief is the result of "a frenzied mind"? (Alma 30:14-16.) Are there not great movements that are sweeping our country declaring as did the anti-Christs of old that they will liberate us from "the foolish ordinances and performances" with which we are bound by a corrupt priesthood? (Alma 30:23.)

Could there be a modern missionary anywhere who has not heard Joseph Smith and the Restoration rejected in the name of Christ and the Bible, just as the ancients rejected Christ himself? Listen to the words of the ancients: "We know that God spake unto Moses: as for this fellow, we know not from whence he is." (John 9:29.) And what of the two men on the Emmaus road that spent a good part of the day with the resurrected Christ with no realization that they were in the presence of God, except as an afterthought? (Luke 24.) Do they not have their modern counterparts both in and out of the Church? And then there was Oliver Cowdery's experience wherein the Lord had to give him a revelation to tell him his prayers had been answered and that he had a testimony. (D&C 6:14-23.)

As long as signs follow them that believe, as long as Satan opposes truth, as long as people continue to be people, and as long as the gospel consists of eternal principles, the experiences of people from one age to the next will be essentially the same. And as long as those experiences are essentially the same, the scriptures in the hands of an able teacher can be brought to life for his students by likening the experiences of peoples of the past to us today.

Testify to Truth of Your Teachings

The divine commission of a gospel teacher includes the responsibility to seal his teachings with personal testimony. In doing so, it is not sufficient for us to merely testify that the gospel is true. Such a statement is axiomatic. Literally, to bear such a testimony is but to testify that truth (the gospel) is true. Our charge is to bear testimony that what we have taught is the gospel, or in other words is true. The Bible could be taken as an illustration of this principle. Great hosts of churches testify that the Bible is true while arguing endlessly over the meaning of its various passages. At issue is not the truth or falsity of the Bible, but rather its true meaning.

The testimony that we bear to the world is not that John truly did see an angel flying through the midst of heaven having the everlasting gospel to preach to those on earth, but rather that the angel has come, that we have that gospel, and that we are

teaching that gospel in fulfillment of that very prophecy. (Rev. 14:6-7.)

The testimony with which Alma concluded his teachings was: "I am commanded to stand and testify unto this people. . . . Behold, I testify unto you that I do know that these things whereof I have spoken are true." (Alma 5:44-45.) Nephi concluded his teachings with this testimony: "I have spoken plainly unto you, that ye cannot misunderstand. And the words which I have spoken shall stand as a testimony against you; for they are sufficient to teach any man the right way; for the right way is to believe in Christ and deny him not; for by denying him ye also deny the prophets and the law." (2 Ne. 25:28.)

Sealing his testimony and establishing the divine pattern for all gospel teachers, Christ said of the Book of Mormon, "As your Lord and your God liveth it is true." (D&C 17:6.) The commission, then, of all gospel teachers is to teach truth and testify that what they have taught is true.

Chapter 3

THE ROLE OF THE GOSPEL TEACHER

My wife's folks used to live in a small farming community. One Sunday morning while we were visiting with them, as my wife and her mother were busy getting our little girls ready for Sunday School, my father-in-law told me what would take place in the adult class that day. He told me what the lesson would be, who the teacher was, what questions he would ask, who would answer the questions, what they would say, and what discussion would ensue.

Having had that preview, I was somewhat amused to sit in class that morning and watch everything happen right on cue. It appeared that each of the class members had an assigned role: there was the questioner, or teacher as he was called; the antagonist, or self-designated scholar; his second; the teacher's helpers; and a large cast without speaking parts. All of them handled their assigned roles with the ease that comes from countless hours of practice. When the buzzer rang signaling the end of the class period, the teacher indicated that they would pick up at the same point the following week, and though I was not present, I am sure they did just that.

In class that morning the assigned lesson was given and all requirements were met. When the class ended, we were right on schedule. One was only left to wonder where we had been and where we were going. That experience, and many similar

ones, have brought me to the conclusion that a teacher who does not have a clearly defined conception of what his role is can easily find himself going through the right motions without going anywhere.

What, then, is the role of the gospel teacher? Some have cast themselves as readers or storytellers, others as entertainers, some as living encyclopedias, and still others, as in the above illustration, as questioners or discussion leaders. With teenage groups some have become sergeants-at-arms, concerned primarily with keeping the roof on the chapel, while with college-age groups some have assumed what they feel to be a more sophisticated approach in which they analyze and challenge basic gospel teachings.

These varying roles assumed by teachers raise fundamental questions about the role of teachers — questions which deserve thoughtful answers. For instance: Should we just accept gospel study as hard work or should we seek ways to make it more fun? Is the primary role of the gospel teacher to dispense information or to motivate action? Is there actually a relationship between stimulating class discussions and real gospel learning? Are there methods and approaches to teaching acceptable in a secular context which are inappropriate for Church classes? Should all teachers subscribe to the same pattern of teaching? Is there a one best way to teach?

May I suggest that the first step in answering such questions is to get a clear perception of the role of a gospel teacher. It is generally agreed that an effective teacher does more than just dispense information, that he or she must be something more than a faceless embodiment of a lesson plan or a conduit through which knowledge is passed from one generation to the next. If teaching were simply a matter of imparting knowledge, there would be no need for teachers beyond the point of teaching people to read, operate tape recorders, and turn the radio and television on and off.

Identifying Needs

The role that the teacher should play is best determined by the overall objectives of the course and the specific objectives

of the individual lessons. In most instances these objectives have been predetermined, and where they have not, the effective teacher will establish them. In either case, the teacher is responsible to determine how to accomplish those objectives and where and when they can and should be appropriately modified for a particular class, group, or individual. Teachers must become sensitive to the fact that no two classes are the same, just as no two students are the same. In a like manner, no two teachers are the same and the manner in which they would approach a lesson could appropriately be as different as their individual experiences. The beginning of effective teaching is in the recognition of those differences. In the final analysis, despite all the efforts of curriculum writers, it is the classroom teacher who must decide what it is that his students will be taught and how they can most effectively be taught.

No better illustration of this principle can be found than the manner in which the Savior taught. When Nicodemus asked him what he needed to do to enter the kingdom of God, he was instructed to be baptized. When a rich young man asked the same question, the answer changed. He was directed to give all that he had to the poor and follow Christ. (See John 3:1-5; Luke 18:18-23.) Suppose you or I had the opportunity to ask the same question of the Savior. What answer would he give us? Would he tell us to be baptized? Certainly not if we have already been baptized. Would he tell us to give all that we have to the poor and follow him? Since most of us have relatively little of this world's goods to give, this seems quite unlikely. What, then, would we be instructed to do? Obviously the answer would be as different as we are different. People are not saved in groups. Salvation is a very personal matter. This being true, our teaching, if it is to be effective, must also be personalized.

Defining Objectives Clearly

To be uncertain as to why we are teaching something is to ensure that our students will be uncertain as to what we have taught. Though there is not necessarily a one best way to teach a particular concept, there must be certainty about what it is that

we are to teach. Vagueness in preparation ensures vagueness in presentation.

To be effective, lessons must be built around concepts that are applicable in the lives of the students. The teacher is responsible to present those concepts in a manner that motivates the students to a course of action that will bring them closer to the Lord. It is suggested, therefore, that after having studied the lesson, the method of presentation could be best decided by asking questions like the following: Why am I teaching this? Does this material have application in the lives of my students? How can I best help them make these concepts a meaningful part of their lives? If we are not satisfied with our answers to these questions, neither we nor our students will be satisfied with our lessons, and we had better continue our search for satisfying answers. The spiritually disciplined teacher will not wait until he is in the classroom to seek inspiration in answering questions of this nature, nor can he wait until Sunday morning or Saturday afternoon to make this kind of preparation.

Controlling the Total Learning Environment

If spiritual learning is to take place, an environment conducive to the presence of the Spirit must exist. It is a primary role of the gospel teacher to establish and maintain that environment. In doing so, it must be recognized that faith and doubt are not compatible classmates; as long as they are allowed to sit next to each other, they will be disruptive to the spirit of the class. The role of the teacher is to bring unity, not only to his class but to all the principles of the gospel. His role is one of synthesis — not analysis. It is not to take apart, but to bring together. It is not to look for flaws but to seek strengths. All too often our attention is centered on that which we cannot understand in preference to that which we cannot misunderstand. The spirit that comes of the Lord is positive, not negative; it brings unity and faith. Its antithesis is discord, derision, and doubt. As President Lee expressed it, the role of the teacher is to put periods instead of question marks after what the Lord has said.

Along with the climate of faith, the atmosphere of the

classroom must be one of trust, in which the shy, the backward, those uncertain of themselves can make inquiries, and express themselves, finding both acceptance and satisfying answers. In many classrooms this means that the teacher must limit or control certain class members who would anxiously dominate class discussion. With younger groups, disruptive students must be controlled in order that others can learn (a matter often not accomplished until their parents are invited to attend class with them). Discussion and questions must also be disciplined in order that they lead toward the accomplishment of the established objectives.

Frequently in the classroom setting a situation will arise spontaneously that catches the attention of the class. A flexible teacher prepared to respond to the needs of his students will capitalize upon such optimum teaching moments. We can only teach what people are willing and ready to learn. In the spontaneous response to the spontaneous situation we often do our most effective teaching. There is, I think, a positive relationship between the frequency of such situations creating themselves and the clarity of objective and purpose in the mind of the inspired teacher.

Enlightening

A teacher should, as Peter expressed it, be ready to give a reason for the hope that is in him. (1 Pet. 3:15.) His role is to instruct, enlighten, edify, direct, and inform. He is a guide on the journey through life, pointing the way back to the presence of God. For him to function only in the role of a facilitator of class discussions, standing on what he perceives to be middle ground, refereeing the battle between truth and error, is for him to abrogate the divine commission that is his. He is the Lord's standard bearer.

Paul, describing the Lord's kingdom, said, "God hath set some in the church, first apostles, secondarily prophets, thirdly teachers, after that miracles, then gifts of healings, helps, governments, diversities of tongues." (1 Cor. 12:28.) Teachers in the Lord's kingdom rank second only to apostles and prophets in prominence and ahead of miracles! They rep-

resent the Lord in that which they teach. They speak at his invitation and in his name. That which they teach should be that which he would teach. Anything that is more or less than this, according to his declaration, "cometh of evil." (3 Ne. 11:40.) Their commission does not embrace the right to speculate or to teach that which is contrary to the divine will. Church classes are not held to facilitate the expression of variant views. The Church is not a forum for social, political, or personal ideologies; it is a forum exclusively for the principles of salvation.

In the context of teaching the gospel to the world, the Lord defined the role of gospel teachers in the following language: "Ye are not sent forth to be taught, but to teach the children of men the things which I have put into your hands by the power of my Spirit; And ye are to be taught from on high. Sanctify yourselves and ye shall be endowed with power, that ye may give even as I have spoken." (D&C 43:15-16.) If the same principles have application when teaching the gospel within the Church, we could summarize the role of the gospel teacher as follows: His calling is to teach the class, not to be taught by the class. This, of course, assumes appropriate preparation on his part. Though he may be edified by the contribution of the class members and learn much in the process of teaching, the essential source of his learning should be his prior preparation and the insight, clarity, and power of conviction he receives from the Holy Ghost as he teaches.

The measure of an effective teacher is not found in his ability to entertain nor in his ability to facilitate stimulating class discussions. To entertain is not necessarily to edify. To involve is not necessarily to enlighten. The education that pertains to the kingdom of God is not play and should not be made to look like play. The divine decree is that we work out our salvation and in many instances that embraces hard, hard work.

Inspiring Gospel Commitment

To stuff the mind with dead knowledge is taxidermy. To expand the soul with purpose and meaning is teaching. The

Lord described his Church as "the only true and living church upon the face of the whole earth." (D&C 1:30.) In a like manner we could say that the principles upon which that Church stands are also both "true" and "living." The real test of our understanding of gospel truths is found in our application of those truths. Gospel principles were not intended for cold storage; they were intended to be lived. To cram the heads of class members with useless information is at least as profitable as loading their stomachs with marbles.

In large measure, the role of the gospel teacher is not to teach truths that are unknown or little understood by the student, but rather to motivate his students to make application of those things that they already know they should be doing. Rarely will the answer as to how that is to be accomplished be found in books or teacher training courses. The answer will grow out of his own experience in living the gospel principle involved and his having so lived that he can respond to the dictates of the Spirit as he studies and teaches.

Evaluating

It has been my observation that good teachers suffer more disappointment and frustration in teaching than do poor teachers. One of the essential differences between those who are teaching effectively and those who are not is their sensitivity to their own successes and failures. There is little hope for improvement or change in a teacher who is unaware of the fact that his lessons have been ineffectual. Commonly, such teachers assume that because the lesson materials were covered, or that because they got the facts across, or that because there was high class involvement and people were intellectually stimulated, they have taught successfully.

To measure with such criteria is to measure with an untrue standard. Studies have shown that juvenile delinquents have a greater knowledge of Bible facts than nondelinquents. There is, therefore, no justification for the assumption that there is a relationship between knowledge and behavior. Where, for instance, is the smoker who has not heard and read about the dangers of smoking? Where is the family in bondage to debt

who has not received repeated warnings about their spending habits? Our prisons are full of people who were very much aware that the course they were pursuing constituted a violation of the law. Hell, in a like manner, will be occupied by those who knew the gospel standard but were not motivated to live it.

Without question, the knowledge of truth is often had independent of the conviction of truth. The ability to verbalize a gospel concept is not necessarily associated with the ability and the desire to live it. Experience has taught me that those who tend to dominate class discussions, giving correct answers, as it were, are most generally those who find the greatest difficulty in making application of the principles involved.

It is a difficult matter to know how effective we have been in our teaching and to what form of feedback we should give listening ear. I am reminded of a former seminary student who when we met years later said, "I didn't like you at the time, but I sure appreciated you when I got on my mission." I have noticed with interest in supervising seminary teachers a reversal of popularity that takes place between the beginning and end of the school year. Consistently, the charismatic storytelling teachers will change places in popularity ratings with those teachers who imposed more spiritual discipline and taught the principles of the gospel. Typically, about February the students tire of personality and start to hunger to be fed.

Feedback from students, fellow teachers, supervisors, and parents are all helpful in evaluating the effectiveness of your teaching. Yet it should be remembered that these sources are not of equal worth. The value to be placed on them becomes a matter of personal judgment. However, the key questions always remain: Have I taught what the Lord would have taught, and did I do it by his Spirit? Did I teach principles that have application in the lives of my students? Did I teach with the conviction that comes from having lived the principles about which I taught? Did I meet student needs, or was I really meeting only my own needs? In short, do I understand my role? Do I know where I have been, and where I am going?

Chapter 4

TEACHING THE FULNESS
OF THE GOSPEL

Although we are told by way of revelation that the Bible and the Book of Mormon contain the "fulness of the gospel," (D&C 42:12), it would be foolish to suppose that because a man had these volumes in his possession that he enjoyed that "fulness." Illustrating this principle Jedediah M. Grant said:

"I am aware that the Christians would think in as much as they circulated the Bible among the nations of the earth, that they have thereby done much towards spreading the Gospel and establishing the kingdom of God, on the earth. But you, as reasonable men, would consider that I reasoned very badly, were I to say that the United States by circulating the Constitution among the various governments on the earth, had thereby established so many republics."[1]

Certainly there is a great difference between the knowledge of freedom and being free. Using another example Elder Grant said:

"Should you light a room with gas, and should an artist make a sketch of the light, and some author write a history of the affair, and at a subsequent date some other man write a history, and should the two accounts be placed together describing the beauty thereof and benefit thereof,

1. *JD*, 4:15.

would the history of the light and the benefit that had been derived therefrom, and the abundance of that light that was said to have existed, light up a hall? If it would, do not buy any more candles, but read the history of candles, and stick that history in your candlesticks; read the history of oil and wick, and stick that in your lamp, and see how much light you will get."[2]

John Taylor suggested that the scriptural records could be likened to a map of our country and the gospel to the country itself. "A man having the map of the United States in his possession," he said, "would be considered foolish if he supposed he possessed the United States; and because a man may have the Old and New Testament in his possession, it does not argue that he has the Gospel." The scriptures, Elder Taylor explained, are "simply records, histories, commandments, etc.," but the gospel "is a living, abiding, eternal and unchangeable principle that has existed co-equal with God, and always will exist, while time and eternity endure, whenever it is developed and made manifest."[3]

A Living Gospel

We have already concluded that teaching the gospel is not just a matter of dispensing information; it is a matter of inspiring reformation. It is the art of directing our students in the realm of personal experience. "Reading the experiences of others, or the revelations given to them," said Joseph Smith, "can never give us a comprehensive view of our condition and true relation to God. Knowledge of these things can only be obtained by experience through the ordinances of God set forth for that purpose."[4] It was not enough for the people of Samaria to hear the testimony of the woman at the well regarding the divinity of Jesus. But after they made their own investigation and had a personal experience, they said, "Now we believe, not because of thy saying: for we have heard him ourselves, and know that this is indeed the Christ, the Savior of the world." (John 4:42.) Knowledge, then, is necessary for spiritual

---

2. *JD*, 4:17.
3. *JD*, 7:362.
4. *HC*, 6:50.

growth; but it is only the prerequisite, the key being personal experience.

This distinction was impressed upon me in a letter from a fellow teacher in which he described his feelings as he completed a series of religion courses during the summer school session at Brigham Young University. He wrote of the fine spirit that had been in his classes and that he felt that he had learned much. Then he expressed his anxiousness to return home saying, "Though I have been edified by that which I have learned, I have missed the spirit that comes from activity and service in the Church."

Another example of this principle is found in the office and calling of a prophet. Harold B. Lee explained: "A prophet . . . does not become a spiritual leader by studying books about religion, nor does he become one by attending a theological seminary. One becomes a prophet, a divinely called religious leader, by actual spiritual contacts. He gets his diploma, as it were, directly from God."[5]

The Missing Link

When I returned from service in the military, one of my relatives said to me: "You were my link with Vietnam. Now that you are safely home, I have lost interest in what is going on over there." So it is with the gospel — we need a link to make it personal. I remember visiting my grandfather, President Joseph Fielding Smith, in his office. When I stood to leave, he got up and walked me to the door. As he did so, he put his arm around my shoulders, looked me in the eye and said, "Remember that you have the blood of prophets in your veins." With that brief but moving salutation he linked me with my ancestry and challenged me to live worthy of that heritage.

On one occasion it was vividly called to my attention that I had failed to provide my students with that link when a student submitted the following written request: "We would like to get to know you better — would you please bear your testimony?" Though I felt that our lessons had been well prepared and well presented, the students had sensed something missing — a

5. *The Improvement Era*, February 1970, p. 94.

personal element — something that was needed to give the lesson life. That testimony had a profound effect on both myself and the students. It provided the personal link that gave life to our subject and united us as a class. Surely this is what the apostle Paul meant when he said, "For our gospel came not unto you in word only, but also in power, and in the Holy Ghost, and in much assurance." (1 Thess. 1:5.)

On another occasion a student asked how he could tell when he had found the right person to marry, in response to which I presented what I thought was an effective discussion on how prayers are answered. At the conclusion of this discussion, another student challenged, "All right, how did all this work for you?" As I shared my personal struggle with the Spirit and eventual answer, the effect was electrifying — we established that link with the principle which made it real.

Competence As a Witness

In the courtroom, competency as a witness is predicated upon knowledge; hearsay testimony is not accepted. So it is in the classroom. The validity of your testimony is based upon the reality of your experience. To change lives you must move from the realm of hearsay to the realm of personal experience. You can teach truth only to the extent that you know truth. You can teach the good life only to the extent that you are living that good life. You can teach about God only to the extent that you know God. The quality of your teaching cannot exceed the quality of your life.

I believe that this was the concept that the Savior was attempting to teach when he told the Nephite nation, "I will declare unto you my doctrine. And this is my doctrine, and it is the doctrine which the Father hath given unto me." (3 Ne. 11:31-32.) It is significant that the Savior declares that the doctrine is his, but also freely acknowledges that he received it from his Father.

This concept can be illustrated with personal standards: I have standards by which I live. They are mine, yet they did not originate with me; I learned them from my father, for they are also his standards. Yet, because I have adopted them as my own, I now refer to them as *my* standards. As I teach them to

my children (which I do primarily by example) I teach what is mine because it is a part of my nature. In a like manner, Paul, in his teaching, used the expression that this is "my gospel," his meaning being that, to the extent that he had learned and lived the gospel, it was his. Presumably, as he used that expression in later years, having grown in faith, he had reference to a larger part of the gospel than he did in his previous references. (Rom. 2:16, 16:25; 2 Tim. 2:8.)

I am reminded of this concept when I see teachers attempt to teach while totally dependent on their notes or outlines. I have wondered how they expect their students to remember what they cannot remember long enough to present. If a lesson has not inspired you, how are you going to teach it in a manner that it will be an inspiration to others? If a concept has not lifted your life, how are you going to teach it so it will lift the lives of your students? Clearly, we cannot give what we do not have, any more than we can come back from where we have not been.

"No man," said Heber J. Grant, "can teach the Word of Wisdom by the Spirit of God who does not live it. No man can proclaim this gospel by the Spirit of the Living God unless that man is living his religion."[6] Your effectiveness as a teacher will not surpass your preparation to teach effectively and your preparation to teach is centered in the way you live. The best of lesson materials will not make a poor teacher a good teacher any more than poor lesson materials will make a good teacher a poor one. The problem is teachers — not syllabus.

Living What We Know

As teachers, we are under no obligation to reveal anything new. Hyrum Smith taught this principle effectively:

> "We have every power and principle to teach the people. Say what God says, and say no more. Never deviate one fraction from what God tells you. . . . Give out the simple principles. A man never fails who only says what he knows; and if any man says more, and can't give reasons, he falls short. Preach the first principles of the Gospel — preach them over again: you will find that day after day new ideas and additional light concerning them

6. *Conference Report,* October 1937, p. 130; hereafter cited as *CR.*

will be revealed to you. You can enlarge upon them so as to comprehend them clearly. You will then be able to make them more plainly understood by those who teach, so that you will meet with scarcely any honest man but will obey them, and none who can oppose."[7]

Often our greatest challenge is to get people to do what they already know they should be doing. I am reminded of the occasion when as a young boy I announced to my father that I was going to exercise my agency and stay home from Church. His response was, "You don't have to go to Church unless you want to. Now get your coat on or you will be late." His philosophy was a good one. I wanted to be in church; I just did not know it at the time, and the only place I would discover it was in church. Brigham Young frequently taught the same concept in reference to those who did not feel like praying. His counsel was that if you do not feel like praying, pray until you do.

The spirit of a principle comes from the application of it, not from the knowledge of it. This is illustrated by the man who came up to President Joseph Fielding Smith after a meeting and said, "That is the first discourse on the Word of Wisdom that I ever liked." President Smith modestly inquired, "Haven't you heard other discourses on the Word of Wisdom?" "Yes," came the reply, "but this is the first one I ever enjoyed. . . . You see, I am keeping the Word of Wisdom now."[8]

Teaching More Than Truth

We conclude, then, that in the highest spiritual sense the fulness of the gospel cannot be found in the scriptures though they bear record of it; rather, it is found in the lives of its adherents. It is spiritual — not intellectual. It consists of power and the witness of the Spirit. In a like manner, the gospel is not merely truth — it is the application of truth. Our charge is greater than just teaching truth; it is to teach the application of truth, for it is only in the application of correct principles that we breathe the breath of life into the gospel and share in its fulness.

7. *HC*, 6:323.
8. *CR*, October 1935, p. 12.

Chapter 5

THE DISCIPLINED TEACHER

A master teacher once suggested that 99 percent of all classroom problems are teacher caused. As startling as this statement seems, upon careful reflection one realizes that many classroom problems can be avoided by the well-disciplined teacher. Taking our attention from the usual discussion of student-centered discipline, let us consider what constitutes a well-disciplined teacher. Three major areas can profitably be considered: first, discipline in preparation; second, discipline in presentation; and third, discipline in conclusion.

Discipline in Preparation

Through revelation the Lord has made it abundantly clear that there is only one acceptable way for us to teach the gospel, and that is by the Spirit. We are familiar with the phrase, "if ye receive not the Spirit ye shall not teach." (D&C 42:14.) We need to constantly remind ourselves, however, that the forepart of that passage states, "The Spirit shall be given unto you by the prayer of faith." (Ibid.) Reference has also been made to the Lord's directive to Hyrum Smith that he seek to obtain the Lord's word before he sought to declare it. This passage takes on added meaning when read in the context in which it was given. The Lord first directed Hyrum to keep the commandments and to do so with all his "might, mind and strength."

(D&C 11:20-22.) Keeping the commandments was a prereq-uisite to his study, which in turn preceded his being granted the power of God unto the convincing of men. The formula for getting the Spirit and having the power to convince men is the prayer of faith, diligence in keeping the commandments, and zeal in gospel study. It is important to realize that gospel knowledge is not dispensed from the heavens solely because of the power of our prayers or the righteousness of our lives. The Lord expects us to study.

The ability to teach effectively can only grow out of a mastery of that which we are to teach. It must be recognized in all preservice and inservice programs that to the extent which we substitute methodology for the substance of that which we are commissioned to teach, we have failed. Significantly, the Lord did not give Hyrum Smith a directive to learn *how* to teach, he told him to learn *what* to teach. Hyrum's knowledge of how to teach was gained in the process of teaching.

This is not to argue that we do away with teacher training programs, but it does suggest that their real value is experienced only by those who pay the price to gain subject mastery. As one teacher expressed it to me: "The single thing that seems to hold me back and suppresses my teaching is a lack of knowledge. As I increase my knowledge, I find my ability to relate the gospel to my students comes naturally. I'm not tied down to someone else's lesson plan made for Joe Everybody, but I have the freedom to put the emphasis where it is needed within the framework of the concepts required in each lesson."

Increased self-confidence will come from the knowledge that you are properly prepared and that you are talking about something that is personally important to your students. This confidence will be sensed by them, but even more important, it will free you from overdependence on the manual or notes and will enable you to center your attention on the students instead of on what you are going to say next. This is important in creating an environment in which you can respond to the Spirit. It enables you to become sensitive to the manner in which your class members are reacting, understanding, or responding to the concepts you are attempting to teach. Your success or failure

will be determined, to a large degree, by the way you react to their responses. This is an ideal spiritual setting for the Holy Ghost to give you direction and inspiration.

The essence of discipline problems is the lack of personal interest on the part of the students. If a lesson has been carefully tailored to meet immediate needs and challenges, and if it is one in which the students can become involved, the basic cause of discipline will have been eliminated. It is particularly difficult to hold the attention of young people when lessons are constructed around concepts that will "help them in their later lives." Our "later lives" are determined by what we do now. Too frequently in our teaching we place the reward of obedience to gospel principles an eternity away. Today is part of eternity. In fact, it is the most important part, for it determines what tomorrow will be.

It is also part of disciplined teaching to realize that each lesson is a part of the whole, and should be presented so that it fits in with the overall objective and purpose of the course of study. Therefore, you must be familiar with the entire course and the relationship of each lesson to the overall objective. Failure to do this often results in the use of motivational ideas, stories, and experiences which would have fit more effectively in another lesson. With a knowledge of what is to be covered in other lessons you can avoid robbing them of their strength. At the same time, each lesson, while accomplishing its own objective, can also be laying the foundation for future lessons. This will also keep you from rushing through certain concepts to touch on things that were going to be treated in greater depth later.

Since it is the teacher's responsibility to respond to the spiritual needs of his class, it may mean occasionally spending more time with certain concepts and hence less time with other concepts than had been originally planned. At the same time, every effort should be made to properly complete each lesson and to complete the entire course of study. The study of the history of the Church, for instance, does not end with the death of the Prophet Joseph Smith or the arrival of the Saints in the Salt Lake Valley, though often we do not get past these events

in our Church history classes. It has been said of one gospel doctrine teacher that he never gets Adam and Eve out of the Garden of Eden. This overemphasis on certain topics does an injustice to the students.

Discipline in Presentation

In the presentation of a lesson there are many opportunities for the undisciplined teacher to be diverted from the path that leads to his objective. Let us consider some of the common temptations which sidetrack teachers. One of these is to say a great deal on matters about which the Lord has said very little. The disciplined teacher has the courage to say, "I don't know," and leave it at that. As President Joseph F. Smith said, "It is no discredit to our intelligence or to our integrity to say frankly in the face of a hundred speculative questions, 'I don't know.' "[1]

This brings us to another danger, that of misquoting. Volumes could be filled with statements supposedly made by the General Authorities which in no way represent what they have said. The disciplined teacher will be sure of his source and will also make every effort to determine if the statement properly represents the doctrine of the Church, or if it is merely the opinion of the author. The *Bishop's Handbook* gives this instruction: "Care should be exercised in accepting any extreme statements, allegedly made by one of the General Authorities, without verifying them with the First Presidency."[2]

The display of irrelevant knowledge also leads away from the accomplishment of your objective. To tell a class everything you know on a subject is not always wise or necessary. It is a good idea to have something in reserve in case someone asks a question. It gets a little uncomfortable to be continually standing at the brink of your knowledge, especially since there is usually someone present who is anxious to entice you to take another step.

Gospel hobbies should also be avoided. On this matter President Joseph F. Smith said that hobbies are dangerous

---

1. *Gospel Doctrine*, 12th ed. (Salt Lake City: Deseret Book, 1961), p. 9; hereafter cited as *GD*.

2. *The Church of Jesus Christ of Latter-day Saints General Handbook of Instructions*, number 20 (The First Presidency, 1968), p. 163.

"because they give undue prominence to certain principles or ideas to the detriment and dwarfing of others just as important, just as binding, just as saving as the favored doctrines or commandments. Hobbies give to those who encourage them a false aspect of the gospel of the Redeemer; they distort and place out of harmony its principles and teachings. The point of view is unnatural. Every principle and practice revealed from God is essential to man's salavation, and to place any one of them unduly in front, hiding and dimming all others, is unwise and dangerous; it jeopardizes our salvation, for it darkens our minds and beclouds our understandings. Such a view, no matter to what point directed, narrows the vision, weakens the spiritual perception and darkens the mind, the result of which is the person thus afflicted with this perversity and contraction of mental vision places himself in a position to be tempted of the evil one, or through dimness of sight or distortion of vision, to misjudge his brethren and give way to the spirit of apostasy. He is not square before the Lord."[3]

Perhaps the greatest temptation of the teacher who is struggling to maintain the attention of his class is to be sensational. There are a number of stories of very questionable origin that are continually being circulated throughout the Church. They usually claim some unverified event for a source and are often based on prophecies supposedly made by Joseph Smith, Heber C. Kimball, or a bishop who had the gift of prophecy. The Three Nephites are often involved and the range of subjects includes such things as politics, the fate of the nation, wealth, famines, the Second Coming, and how many presidents of the Church there will be.

These stories have no place in the classrooms of the Church. When the Lord has such information for us, it will come from the prophet and will be dispensed through proper priesthood channels. Appropriate counsel is continually being given to the Church by its leaders — counsel which the properly prepared teacher will be familiar with. Careful attention should be given to the messages of the General Authorities in

3. *GD*, pp. 116-17.

stake and general conferences. The *Ensign, New Era,* and other Church publications should be read regularly. Stability and testimony are not built on sensational stories; they come by following the prophet and living the gospel. Meaningful attention will be accorded to the teacher who establishes the reputation of being orthodox and sound in doctrine.

One teaching method in which teacher discipline is extremely important, but perhaps most commonly lacking, is that of class discussion. Because they stimulate personal involvement, class discussions can be, when properly conducted, an excellent teaching tool. The art of disciplining class discussions will be considered in the next chapter.

Discipline in Conclusion

Discipline in concluding a lesson is essential to its success. Nothing agonizes a class like the teacher who does not know when to quit. It takes a special kind of courage and discipline to cut part of a lesson, particularly when much effort has gone into its preparation, but the wise teacher knows his time limit and keeps it.

In concluding a lesson, care should be taken not to exaggerate the importance of the concept considered. Temperance should be used in the use of superlatives and the making of promises that will be enjoyed as a result of the application of a particular principle. Each lesson should be kept in perspective with the entire gospel plan. At the same time, it should be emphasized that the gospel is positive — not negative. The conclusion to a lesson should always consist of an expression of encouragement, faith, and testimony.

Chapter 6

DISCUSSIONS:
LEADING OR BEING LED?

No teaching device has been more abused in Church classrooms than group discussions. At their worst they represent little more than uncontrolled debates or group arguments. Such discussions do much to foster the spirit of contention and hurt feelings, and to challenge faith rather than build it. When improperly conducted, class discussions frequently alienate the Spirit and are at variance with sound doctrine.

In contrast, few teaching devices have been more effective in stimulating personal involvement, facilitating the sharing of faith-promoting experiences, and enhancing group and individual commitment to living gospel standards. If scriptural sanction is needed for the use of group discussions, it can be found in the Lord's instructions to the School of the Prophets. "Appoint among yourselves a teacher," the revelation reads, "and let not all be spokesmen at once; but let one speak at a time and let all listen unto his sayings, that when all have spoken that all may be edified of all, and that every man may have an equal privilege." (D&C 88:122.) Let us then center our attention on appropriate guidelines to ensure that group discussions conducted under our direction will foster spiritual learning and gospel commitment.

Discussion Leadership

Inspired classes are not the result of uninspired preparation. The Spirit of the Lord is not the reward of indolence. This
principle is true in all dimensions of teaching. A teacher can no
more substitute a class discussion for personal preparation than
he can satisfy his hunger by reading a menu. Preparation is as
important to the success of a class discussion as it is to any other
part of lessons. Typically, teachers who are inexperienced or
unsure of themselves will use class discussions as an attempt to
shift the burden of teaching to members of the class whom he
may regard as more knowledgeable than himself.

To draw upon the knowledge or experience of class members is always appropriate; to abrogate your role as a teacher for
that of a moderator is never appropriate. All too often when the
teacher surrenders his role of leadership in the learning process,
the class discussion degenerates to the point where it becomes
little more than a smorgasbord of prejudice and ignorance. In
such discussions, conclusions or lasting impressions are often
made by the most vocal or influential members of the class,
irrespective of their spiritual validity.

The teacher who has not properly prepared himself and the
class for a group discussion could be likened to a chemistry
professor going into the chemistry laboratory and throwing a
catalyst into a large vat of unknown chemicals, and then step-
ping back to watch the reaction with the hope that some chemi-
cal union that will be beneficial to mankind will take place.
Having done so, he invites his students to freely take home
whatever quantities of the concoction they desire with the
appended hope that it will be a help to them in their later lives.

The chance that a scientific contribution will be made by
such methods is very small. In fact, the possibility that something negative will result from the experiment is at least as great
as the possibility that something positive will result. Certainly
the same principle is true for the unplanned and uncontrolled
class discussion.

The skillful teacher brings knowledge to be shared and
expanded upon — not just memorized — and few teaching tools

are more suited to this process than are appropriately led class discussions. Students must become more than depositories of teacher knowledge. Tape recorders do not think; they do not serve missions, raise families, or preside in the organizations of the Church; and they do not get saved in the kingdom of God.

The inspired teacher, therefore, must do more than dispense knowledge. He must lead his students in the experience of confronting and contrasting, weighing and balancing, contemplating and meditating. He must help them absorb and grasp; he must guide them into the experience of transformation and regeneration. He leads with confidence, for he charted the course and knows the way. He has assessed the strength of the group and knows the time available for the journey. He will have oriented all participants as to where they are going, what their purposes are, the necessary safety rules, and the limits and bounds of the journey. He will see that discipline is imposed upon those who race ahead of the group and patience exercised for stragglers who have trouble keeping up.

Discussions with Purpose

All topics for discussion are not equally appropriate. In the selection of discussion topics the following factors should be considered:

1. Will it lead to the accomplishment of the objectives of the course, lesson, or purpose for which the group is meeting?
2. Is the issue under consideration significant and timely?
3. Is the discussion of the issue within the range of the knowledge and competence of those with whom it is to be discussed?
4. Is the issue one which would require more time for satisfactory discussion and study than its importance merits?
5. Is the discussion one which will result in increased testimony and spiritual conviction?
6. Do the scriptures or have the Brethren enunciated a clear position on the matter? Does it place us in a position of clarifying what the Lord has not?

A class discussion can be an effective method of teaching the skills of problem-solving. It can also be helpful to the students in clarifying views and formulating attitudes. Such discussions are often introduced with thought-provoking questions or quotations. The case-study method or open-ended stories can be used effectively for this purpose. These can be real or hypothetical situations that create a problem situation to which the class is invited to respond.

As the class struggles with the problem you, as the teacher, will have the opportunity to test their understanding and to assess the extent to which what you are teaching is solidifying and being synthesized in their minds. The value of correct answers is appreciably lessened if they are predicated on poor or faulty reasoning. Class discussions provide the opportunity to explore the strength of reasons or depth of understanding behind responses. They also provide the opportunity to reinforce gospel teachings and act as springboards to teach related concepts. Nonverbal members of the class should be involved in order that their level of understanding might also be tested and positive reinforcement given to them.

Unified Search for Truth

In a class discussion the group's purpose is not to establish eternal truths, but rather to identify those truths and clarify their application in everyday living. The great question of the preexistent council was "Whom shall I send?" not "What shall I do?" God seeks no counsel from man as to what the plan of salvation should be. Properly, the purpose of class discussions should not be to defend a particular position or theory, but rather to seek truth. Certainly, it should be understood by all participating that truth is not determined by conducting an opinion poll. As the Lord said: "For my thoughts are not your thoughts, neither are your ways my ways. . . . For as the heavens are higher than the earth, so are my ways higher than your ways, and my thoughts than your thoughts." (Isa. 55:8-9.) Expressing the same idea, Brigham Young said, "One scriptural proof is worth ten thousand opinions."[1]

---

1. *HC*, 3:396.

Sources of Authority

As the group searches for understanding, no question is of greater importance than that of where they should look. On any matter of importance one can easily find a great variety of opinion; such is the case even within the Church. Not infrequently Church members will shop for opinions, going from one source of authority to another until they find someone who will say what they want to hear. Often the answers that are given to questions serve only to measure the spiritual maturity of those giving them. Again, the purpose of class discussions is not to find justification for a particular view, nor is it to facilitate the expression of private views. The purpose of a class discussion is to bring the combined experience and understanding of the group to bear on the matter of identifying and clarifying the mind and will of the Lord. Such being the case, the primary sources of authority should be those through which he has and does express his will. They would include the following:

1. The teachings of the Prophet Joseph Smith, for the Lord said of him, "This generation [meaning dispensation] shall have my word through you." (D&C 5:10.)

2. Our living prophet, for the constitution of this Church is not a revelation or a compilation of revelations. We have a living constitution which consists of the First Presidency of the Church, who have the right to preside over all of the Church's affairs, both temporal and spiritual.

3. The General Authorities of the Church, as that which they say represents the united voice of their respective quorums.

4. The scriptures, our standards of measurement in all things.

5. Our local priesthood leaders, men charged with the responsibility to institute Church programs on a local basis and to act as judges in Israel.

6. Our parents, for the family is the basic unit of eternity, and none are more qualified to counsel than inspired fathers and mothers.

As appropriate, other sources of help in problem solving might include:

1. Men and women of faith and judgment.
2. Friends who have sound judgment.
3. Good books.

Cautions

Since it is the responsibility of the teacher to see that the discussion accomplishes its desired end, he should be prepared to tactfully, and yet authoritatively, correct erroneous ideas that develop during the discussion. In order to do this, it is wise to anticipate trends of thought that might be brought up which are not harmonious with the gospel and consider how they could most effectively be directed to correct conclusions. An important caution at this point, however, is that the teacher avoid overplanning. A discussion too rigidly controlled will thwart spontaneity and creativity. Many good discussions are ruined by teachers who turn them into a guessing game to see if the students can choose the words or phrase that the teacher has chosen to convey a particular thought or concept. When this happens, insightful student responses are often thwarted with a "That's not quite what I had in mind."

The lifeblood of class discussions is the flexibility that enables the teacher to respond to the needs, interests, experiences, and understanding levels of his class. Oftentimes in the course of discussions it will become evident that lesson objectives need to be modified or changed. It is in such a context that optimum teaching moments are most often found.

Since class discussions do result in high involvement, they can be plagued with the problem of overemotion. Such emotion may be of value when a bear is chasing you, but its effect in class discussions is usually to restrict individual ability to reason and to think clearly. People who have become defensive or who feel that they are being pitted against the teacher do little or no constructive learning. The key to avoiding overemotion rests in the unity of purpose that should be the actuating force of class discussions. In the context of Church classrooms, group discussions should be held for no other purpose

than that of a cooperative search for truth and understanding.

The best rule, then, for effective class discussion is the exercise of courtesy for class members and their expressions. The teacher has no responsibility to comment on everything that others say and certainly he and the class members should avoid being critical and judgmental. Truth is taught in a positive, not a negative, manner. Informality will usually facilitate the discussion, as will the suggestion to the talkative members of the class that they limit their expressions in deference to those from whom the class does not hear as often.

As a summary to these cautions and to this chapter it is stressed that the only justification for a class discussion is that it lead to the accomplishment of your objective. If that is not its purpose, it is without purpose. When properly used, class discussions will supplement your lessons, not supplant your teaching. You help ensure accomplishment of that end through careful selection of a topic, clearly defined objectives, well-established bounds and limitations, and personal preparation to give the discussion meaningful direction or redirection as necessary. A skillful teacher would no more leave a class discussion without a conclusion than a guide would abandon his charges in the middle of a wilderness trek. Summaries of principles learned, conclusions as to what principles of truth are, and testimony to the truth are always appropriate conclusions to class discussions.

Chapter 7

SPIRITUAL KNOWLEDGE:
LEARNED OR EARNED?

Significant learning is self-learning. Learning takes place when we want to learn, are ready to learn, and are willing to work to learn. Only in the context of these three variables can the teacher extend meaningful help; and even then, the process is student- not teacher-centered. The learning process is illustrated in the manner in which babies learn to walk. Suppose that the child's mother carefully explained the process in which the muscles and sinews operate to pull and push in order to work the jointed mechanisms called feet, ankles, and knees. Then suppose she showed the child what he must do with his spine, how to best hold his arms, explained the principle of balance, gave the child assignments, established a deadline by which he was to master the basic skills of walking, and briefly reviewed the actions on which he would be tested.

The example, of course, is nonsensical; yet it effectively points out that a knowledge of the process of learning is not necessary for learning to take place, and that learning is student-centered. The Savior, teaching the importance of spiritual birth, did not attempt an explanation of the process, but merely announced: "The wind bloweth where it listeth, and thou hearest the sound thereof, but canst not tell whence it cometh, and whither it goeth: so is every one that is born of the Spirit." (John 3:8.) Effectually, the Savior is saying the

process of gaining spiritual knowledge is indefinable. Like the process of physical growth, you cannot see it take place, yet in the process of time you can see that it has taken place. The author of Ecclesiastes expressed the same concept in this language: "Thou knowest not what is the way of the spirit, nor how the bones do grow in the womb of her that is with child: even so thou knowest not the works of God who maketh all." (Eccles. 11:5.)

A technical knowledge of how we walk is of no relevance in teaching babies to walk. In fact, we do not teach babies to walk; they learn by themselves, doing so in their own time and in their own way. The mother's role, or that of the teacher, though important, is limited to giving encouragement and support. She puts the child on the floor, takes care to see that he does not hurt himself, and gives him love as she reinforces his efforts. She may steady him as he gains a sense of balance, and then holding his arms she may introduce him to the process of placing one foot before the other, but that is the extent of her role. Gradually, in the course of weeks, the child gains a sense of balance, learns to stand alone, and then step by step begins to walk.

The process of learning to speak is much the same. The child, finding himself in an environment where there is speaking, where he is addressed and invited to take part, gradually learns to do so. The learning process is not appended to theories, methods, and schedules. Again, the analogy is a natural one for use in illustrating the manner in which we learn the language of the Spirit. Conversance in that language does not come from theories, methods, and schedules. In fact, we have a very limited ability to explain how it does come, but gradually, "line upon line, precept upon precept, here a little and there a little," it comes. (2 Ne. 28:30.) It grows out of an environment in which the language is spoken, in which the learner is addressed in that language, and in which he is invited to take part. It is a process in which people must do their own learning.

The commandment is "save yourselves." (D&C 38:42.) You can no more work out another man's salvation than you can

learn to walk for him or learn to speak for him. We cannot make someone grow spiritually any more than we can make them grow physically. We can provide an environment that is conducive to spiritual growth, just as we provide an environment that is conducive to physical growth, but we cannot trigger the processes of growth.

To All a Needful Portion

We can only teach that which our students are prepared to receive. Contrary to common misconception, if we do not know much, our capacity to learn is not very great. We can only learn in relation to what we already know. The more we know, the greater is our capacity to learn. The less we know, the less is our capacity to learn.

I served as a chaplain in the military and in that capacity was expected in many instances to act in a nondenominational role. Before I went to Vietnam, I was concerned with the question of how I would minister to the needs of those who were not members of our Church. Suppose, for example, I was called upon to minister to a Catholic or Protestant on the battlefield. Should I administer to him by the power of the Priesthood, or should I just pray for him, or read to him from the scriptures as his own minister would do? Many variations of this question occurred to me.

I found, however, that it resolved itself rather simply. You take a person as far as his faith permits you to take him. In fact, the Lord had announced the principle in the scriptures — I just needed to find it. He said, "Treasure up in your minds continually the words of life, and it shall be given you in the very hour that portion that shall be meted unto every man." (D&C 84:85.) If a man had faith in the power of the Priesthood, I would exercise that Priesthood. If he had faith in prayer, I would pray. If all I could do was to reassure him, then I would give him that "needful portion." In a like manner, as a teacher I can come to a class with a five-gallon bucket full of knowledge but if my students come with cups, though I empty my bucket, all they can take away is what their cups will hold.

This principle is basic to all teaching situations. The

teacher cannot exceed the spiritual maturation level of his students any more than he could exceed their physical maturation level. Spiritual maturity comes in the course of time as we work to gain it. Christ is our prototype. The scriptures tell us that he advanced from grace to grace, gradually increasing in wisdom, stature, and favor with God. (D&C 93:12-17; Luke 2:52.) As Paul put it, Christ learned obedience by the things which he suffered and thus became perfect. (Heb. 5:8-9.)

One of the greatest gospel doctrine courses ever taught was that taught by Christ to the righteous remnant of the Nephite nation. At the end of the first day of class, Christ assessed the understanding of this select group of students and said, "I perceive that ye are weak, that ye cannot understand all my words which I am commanded of the Father to speak unto you at this time." He then directed his students to return to their homes and study what they had been taught. As part of their homework assignment they were directed to seek understanding in prayer in order that they might comprehend what he, the Master Teacher, had taught. They were further directed to prepare their minds for what they would be taught the next day in class. (3 Ne. 17:2-3.) Clearly, the Savior shifted the burden of responsibility to his students.

Learning Is Earned

As there is no strength in food that is not eaten, there are no blessings in commandments that are not lived. To "just about" live the commandments is to "just about" receive the blessings. In the realm of spiritual things there are no unearned blessings. The Lord has said: "Let every man be diligent in all things. And the idler shall not have place in the church, except he repent and mend his ways." (D&C 75:29.) Again, the principle is as true in the realm of acquiring spiritual learning as it is in the sphere of temporal possessions. It is no more the desire of the Lord to have people emotionally and spiritually dependent on others, or the Church, than it is to have them so dependent in the realm of temporal things. With inspired insight, Elder Boyd K. Packer pointed out: "There are too many in the Church who seem to be totally dependent, emotionally

and spiritually, upon others. They subsist on some kind of emotional welfare. They are unwilling to sustain themselves. They become so dependent that they endlessly need to be shored up, lifted up, endlessly need encouragement, and they contribute little of their own."[1]

The concern expressed by Elder Packer is that if we lose emotional and spiritual self-reliance, we are weakened as much and perhaps more than when we become dependent materially. Counsel and advice, he said, should not be doled out without consideration of the individual's ability to solve his own problems or gain the necessary help in his own home. Only when those resources are inadequate should he turn to the Church. The power to receive individual revelation is easily lost.

Teaching Self-Reliance

The principle of self-reliance has many important implications for the teaching of the gospel. In fact, real learning begins at the point that we assume personal responsibility for our learning. If there is a single moment of maturity, it is the moment at which we realize that the burden is ours to learn and not the teacher's to teach. I have heard it said that the strength of our country's most prestigious graduate schools is that they leave their students alone. I recall the feelings of frustration and disappointment that I felt in my own graduate program because I was not getting what I desired to get from my professors. Satisfaction did not come until I came to the realization that it was up to me to get what I wanted. The distinction is the same as that of giving a hungry man a fish rather than teaching him how to fish. The gospel seeks for lasting solutions.

A few years ago I gave five classes of seminary students, all of them high school seniors, their final examination in the form of a take-home test on the first day of the final quarter. The students were to complete the exam and return it at their convenience and were promised that any help they needed in completing it would be eagerly given. I explained that the exam was in large measure a maturity test to see if they could complete it without constant reminders and a deadline. Three of the

---

1. *Ensign*, August 1975, p. 86.

153 students involved completed the test on their own. The rest waited until the seminary principal ordered me to capitulate to their terms; a deadline, an extended deadline, frequent cajoling, and calls to their mothers. In their educational experience to that point, these students had not assumed any meaningful personal responsibility.

The natural tendency to avoid personal responsibility in the learning process is illustrated in the typical teacher-student question and answer exchange. Though they are not always conscious of it, most teachers develop dependency relationships with certain vocal students whom they can always depend on to answer questions and carry the class discussion. If those students, usually two or three in number, were all absent at the same time, a strange silence would descend upon the class.

The situation results from the teacher's natural dislike of the awkward uncertainty of seeking responses from the noncontributors who would rather say that they do not know than allow someone to publicly probe their understanding and possibly embarrass them. If the teacher's question calls for a factual answer, his helpers in the older classes or the "goodie-goodie" in the younger classes can usually be depended upon to supply the answer. If, instead, the teacher asks a concept question that requires some real thought, he will either receive no response or a very superficial response. To think is work, and few people are going to work if they do not have to. All too frequently, questions worth asking are not asked because the class has taught the teacher that they will not be answered.

To get meaningful answers to questions, the teacher must either endure a silence that becomes more painful than the thought process, thus forcing mental involvement; or pursue it by placing his students on the spot to respond and refusing to accept lazy thinking. Clever students will bait the teacher, through feigning ignorance, into asking successively easier questions until he finds that he has answered his own question or the student has answered a question that requires no thought. The quality of the responses the teacher receives will rarely exceed the standard he is willing to accept. A usual part of such discussions is the "Don't ask us, you're the teacher" response.

Yet if we are to accept the principle of self-reliance, the role of the teacher becomes that of helping the students help themselves. It must be recognized that we cannot learn for them. The teacher who knows all the answers and who can solve all the problems for his students fails to realize that in that process he often weakens rather than strengthens them.

Measuring Success

In the long term, a teacher has succeeded when his students no longer need him. The responsibility of parents is to prepare their children for the time when they leave home and commence a family of their own. Meddling parents or parents who have created a dependency relationship with their children are a primary cause of unhappiness and failure in their children's marriages. The gospel standard is to teach correct principles in order that people might be able to govern themselves. The principle is the same whether we speak of parents, ecclesiastical leaders, counselors, or teachers. In each instance their purpose should be to so teach that those being instructed know correct principles and have the faith and confidence to make application of those principles. Their role is to help those under their direction gain a sense of balance, learn to stand on their own, and to walk with confidence.

Chapter 8

EXCELLENCE IN GOSPEL TEACHING

Excellence in gospel teaching is attained by teachers who have a deep respect for the profundity of the gospel and who, having experienced the reality of the gospel, have prepared themselves to teach a real gospel to real people. It has been correctly observed that you can be no greater as a teacher than you are as a person. Great teachers are great because they *are* something, not because they have *read* something. Great books will never replace good teaching. If the answer to effective learning is found solely in the text material, then from the time people learn to read there is no justification for teachers, classrooms, schools, or universities; we need only writers and libraries. But good teachers are harder to find than good books — and are capable of doing things that books cannot. The difference between a great book and a great teacher is the difference between a letter from a loved one and the actual companionship of that loved one. It is the difference between hearing about great experiences and having great experiences.

Great teachers bring color, tone, and meaning to that which we read and have experienced. From them we catch something; we sense their commitment, feel their excitement, are lifted by their dedication, refreshed through their insights, encouraged by their struggles, and strengthened by their tes-

timonies. As the scriptures declare, an atmosphere is created in which the teacher and student "understand one another, and both are edified and rejoice together." (D&C 50:22.)

Reverence for Gospel Principles

Our commitment to and love for gospel principles cannot extend beyond our knowledge of those principles. We all have many "How are you?" acquaintances, with whom we exchange greetings and about whom we know enough to show some personal interest. These are not the people, however, to whom we turn when we seek important counsel, need help, or are faced with a crisis. In such instances, we turn to that limited sphere of close friends whom we know well and feel comfortable with.

So it is with gospel principles. Many are able to call them by name and converse about them, but their association is not close enough that they think to turn to them in time of need. Typical of such an association are students who, after completing a course in the Book of Mormon, for instance, go out saying, "Well, now we have had Book of Mormon — what else is there?" Somehow they went through a Book of Mormon course without forming any association; they missed the greatness, the vastness, the depth, the beauty, and the true meaning of the book. Instead of beginning an association with a great volume of scripture, they have completed one.

Excellence in gospel teaching takes place when a teacher has brought a meaning to and taught a respect for gospel principles, resulting in lifelong associations. Like good marriages, they are the kinds of relationships that quietly deepen and grow with the passing of years as the challenges and experiences of life are faced.

Learning by Faith

The respect we teach for gospel principles must also embrace the manner in which we study those principles. Frequently people will come to me with the question, "How do you study the scriptures?" having in mind that I will give them some secret formula that will greatly increase their ability to assimi-

late and retain. Their attention is centered on such questions as "Should I study in the morning or in the evening?" "Should I have an established time and place for study?" "Should I study topically or chronologically?" In response to such inquiries, I have attempted to explain that the answer to effective gospel study is not found in the mechanics of study. Although some systems may be more effective than others, it is essentially a matter of personal preference. The answer to effective gospel study is not found in the methodology of study; it is of little consequence if we mark with a red pencil or a blue one. What does matter, however, is the attitude with which we study.

The Lord said that we should "seek learning, even by study and also by faith." (D&C 88:118.) This raises the interesting question as to how you gain knowledge by faith. The answer is significant. Suppose, for instance, that I go off to school and gain a mastery in a particular field of study and then return to measure the gospel by the standards of my academic training. Would the conclusions that I arrived at be the same as those I would arrive at if I started from the premise that the gospel was true and measured my academic training by the gospel standard? In the first instance I could easily find myself setting aside those parts of the gospel that did not square with my academic training; in the second instance, I would find myself setting aside those parts of my academic training that did not square with the gospel. The results would be appreciably different.

To study the Old and New Testaments from the perspective that Joseph Smith was, in fact, a prophet, and that the Book of Mormon, the Doctrine and Covenants, and the Pearl of Great Price are also scripture, flavors or markedly changes virtually every conclusion that we arrive at. Consistently such conclusions will provide a sharp contrast with the rest of the Christian world. In fact, if we study from the perspective of that faith, we find ourselves in the position of saying to the world that we are the stewards of the interpretation of the Old and New Testaments and that they can never understand them independent of Mormonism. We are saying that the truth of the gospel cannot be had independent of a knowledge and testimony of our living prophets. Ultimately, that contention

must rest on the foundation of faith — for it can rest nowhere else.

Loyalty to Correct Principles

"The opinions of men," stated the Prophet Joseph Smith, "are to me as the crackling of thorns under the pot, or the whistling of the wind."[1] Expounding a truth about Deity that was in opposition to Christian tradition, he challenged: "I defy all the learning and wisdom and all the combined powers of earth and hell together to refute it."[2]

Joseph Smith, the master teacher of our dispensation, made no attempt to reconcile what he taught with popularly held tenets. "The object with me," he avowed, "is to obey and teach others to obey God in just what He tells us to do. It matters not whether the principle is popular or unpopular, I will always maintain a true principle, even if I stand alone in it."[3] He boldly set forth his position, stating, "The great designs of God in relation to the salvation of the human family, are very little understood by the professedly wise and intelligent generation in which we live."[4]

Revelation is the only legitimate source for true religion. On that subject Joseph Smith said, "I break the ground; I lead the way. . . ." Illustrating his point, he told a story about a banquet to which Christopher Columbus was invited and given the seat of honor.

"A shallow courtier present, who was meanly jealous of him, abruptly asked him whether he thought that in case he had not discovered the Indies, there were not other men in Spain who would have been capable of the enterprize? Columbus made no reply, but took an egg and invited the company to make it stand on end. They all attempted it, but in vain; whereupon he struck it upon the table so as to break one end, and left it standing on the broken part,

---

1. *HC*, 5:402.
2. *HC*, 6:306.
3. *HC*, 6:223.
4. *HC*, 4:595.

illustrating that when he had once shown the way to the new world nothing was easier than to follow it."[5]

Mormonism is not built upon any other foundation than that of a living faith and living revelation. It does not follow the world nor seek approval from it. We have all the truth the Christian world possesses, and, as Joseph Smith said, "an independent revelation in the bargain," and God will bear us off triumphant.[6] Excellence in gospel teaching demands loyalty of the gospel teacher to those revealed principles. And though the teacher should be prepared to give reason for that faith which is in him, he has no obligation to answer every question and objection that can be raised. As Ezra Taft Benson said, "Every man eventually is backed up to the wall of faith, and there he must make his stand."[7]

Loyalty to truth demands that the teacher be discriminating in the sources he uses. He would be embarrassed to discover that he had perpetuated myth, for he realizes that faith is not built on falsehoods or sensationalism. He accepts his task to separate the wheat from the chaff. He finds it wisdom and sound practice to be accurate in his scholarship and to teach only those doctrines and use only those stories about which he is certain. He is cautious not to embellish lessons with questionable or hearsay-type information. He does not teach with a bag of tricks or a file full of gospel "secrets" and a "wait until you hear this" attitude. He will not prostitute the gospel or sell his soul for classroom popularity. He recognizes the inherent danger in having his own loyal following instead of having students loyally following principles of truth.

Adapting to People

Excellence in gospel teaching is found when an application of eternal verities is made to mundane realities, realities which vary from place to place and from person to person. If we are really going to teach people instead of lessons, we must

---

5. *HC*, 5:402.
6. *HC*, 6:479.
7. *Ensign*, May 1975, p. 65.

begin where those people honestly are. For far too long we have begun lessons and courses at a point where we fondly hoped our students were or where our faulty memories supposed we were. As Victor Frankl observed in his vividly insightful account of life in the Jewish death camps during the second World War, "It was the incorrigible optimists who were the most irritating companions."[8]

As we struggle to gain our freedom from the prisons of doubt and sin, little help is extended by teachers who ooze with lofty platitudes, handling the frustrations and heartaches of life with a glib "Everything will be all right," or "Pray about it and you will know." Everything has not always worked out just right, even for the faithful Saints, and answers to prayers are often hard to come by, even for prophets. I have heard scores of talks and lessons which center in Nephi's great statement that the Lord gives no commandments that he does not prepare a way for us to accomplish the thing which he commands. (1 Ne. 3:7.) I am yet to hear someone take as a text the statement of the Lord that when he gives a commandment to do a work, and we attempt to do it with all our might and strength, and we cease not to be diligent in the accomplishment of that work and yet we are prevented from accomplishing it, that "it behooveth [him] to require that work no more at the hands of those sons of men, but to accept of their offerings." (D&C 124:49.) Nephi, with all his greatness, never was able to convert Laman and Lemuel. Sometimes we just do the best we can and leave the matter in the hands of the Lord.

Suffice it to say that meaningful lessons can rarely be developed separate from or in isolation of the people for whom they are intended or the conditions in which those people live. Excellence in gospel teaching comes when our view is toward the heavens and our feet are firmly on the ground. It is teaching that is flexible and adaptable to the needs of those we teach, in both the planning and the presentation. It is always a temptation to teach to meet our own needs and not those of our students, or for the class to talk about how principles apply to people other than themselves. We frequently give excellent

8. *Man's Search for Meaning* (New York: Washington Square Press, 1967), p. 53.

answers to questions no one is asking and offer good counsel for problems no one has, while remaining blind to existent needs.

Toward Spiritual Excellence in Teaching

The answer to excellence in gospel teaching is not found in methodology. A mastery of methods does not make an inspired teacher. For that matter, we are yet to determine what methods most effectively facilitate the learning process. Little is done in the field of education today on the basis of objective data. We have no consistent body of research that indicates to us that teaching methods make a difference. As Wallen and Travers observed in their *Handbook of Research on Teaching,* "there is hardly any evidence to favor one method over another."[9]

For instance, in eighty-eight independent comparisons of the lecture and discussion methods reported in thirty-six experimental studies, 51 percent favored the lecture method and 49 percent favored the discussion method.[10] Stephens, in another study, concluded after looking at the research reported that they could not find anything that made a difference in teaching effectiveness.[11] Research studies have indicated that teachers in the public schools are no more effective in bringing about student learning than are untrained persons of comparable intelligence and general education. It has been observed that the "rating of teaching skill, whether supplied by administrators, pupils, or a visiting mother-in-law, are notoriously inaccurate."[12]

Further, it has been found that there are no consistent relationships between teacher characteristics and effectiveness in teaching.[13] There is no more a common denominator by which skillful teachers can be identified than there is one by which we identify intelligence, wit, personality, or spirituality.

---

9. N. E. Wallen, and R. M. W. Travers, "Analysis and Investigation of Teaching Methods," *Handbook of Research on Teaching,* ed. N. L. Gage (Chicago: Rand McNally, 1963), p. 484.

10. *Critical Issues in Educational Psychology,* ed. Meredith D. Gall and Beatrice A. Ward (Boston: Brown and Co., 1974), pp. 210-12.

11. Ibid.

12. Ibid., pp. 218-19.

13. Orville G. Brim, Jr., *Sociology and the Field of Education* (New York: Russell Sage Foundation, 1958), p. 32.

Attempts to identify teachers by character traits brings to mind Greenwalt's observation on leadership studies when he remarked that "most recitals of executive virtues sound, as a matter of fact, rather like the *McGuffey Readers* or those little cards which pop out of penny scales certifying that the customer is loyal, trustworthy, kind, honest, generous, and weighs 198 pounds."[14]

Excellence in gospel teaching does not result from the mastery of some arbitrarily determined set of criteria, nor is it inherent in some combination of personality traits. The ability to teach is a spiritual gift, granted by the Spirit of God in accordance with the same eternal principles by which all spiritual gifts are given. (Moroni 10:9-10.) "Are all apostles?" Paul asked. "Are all prophets? are all teachers? are all workers of miracles?" (1 Cor. 12:29.) The answer, of course, is that they are not. "For all have not every gift given unto them. . . . To some is given one, and to some is given another." (D&C 46:11, 12.) The command is that we seek earnestly the best gifts.

For a man to seek the gift of teaching is wholly appropriate, but it should not be supposed that spiritual gifts are granted for the completion of training courses. If such was the case, we should have training courses in healing, prophecy, working miracles, speaking in tongues, and so forth. This is not to say that training courses are without purpose or that they should be avoided, for certainly they can be a part of the seeking process. Yet it must be realized that as the gospel and the commission to teach are divine gifts, so is the ability to teach the gospel. Such gifts follow devotion, faith, and obedience on the part of man. Their receipt is always predicated upon obedience to laws — laws which can only be fully taught by teachers who know and live them.

---

14. Crawford H. Greenwalt, *The Uncommon Man* (New York: McGraw-Hill Book Co., 1959), p. 61.

INDEX